modern readers   stage 1

The Big River

Vera Abi Saber

To Betty...
for her guidance and friendship.

Richmond

© VERA ABI SABER, 2005

Richmond

Diretoria: *Paul Berry*
Gerência editorial: *Sandra Possas*
Coordenação de arte: *Christiane Borin*
Coordenação de revisão: *Estevam Vieira Lédo Jr.*
Coordenação de produção gráfica: *André Monteiro, Maria de Lourdes Rodrigues*
Coordenação de produção industrial: *Wilson Troque*

Projeto editorial: *Kylie Mackin*

Assistência editorial: *Gabriela Peixoto Vilanova*
Revisão: *Denise Ceron*
Projeto gráfico de miolo e capa: *Ricardo Van Steen Comunicações e Propaganda Ltda./Oliver Fuchs*
Edição de arte: *Christiane Borin*
Ilustrações de miolo e capa: *Dave Santana*
Diagramação: *Formato Comunicação*
Pré-impressão: *Hélio P. de Souza Filho, Marcio H. Kamoto*
Impressão e acabamento: *BMF Gráfica e Editora*
Lote: 270757

Dados Internacionais de Catalogação na Publicação (CIP)
(Câmara Brasileira do Livro, SP, Brasil)

Saber, Vera Abi
  The big river / Vera Abi Saber. — São Paulo : Richmond Publishing, 2004. — (Modern readers ; stage 1)

  Vários ilustradores

  1. Inglês (Ensino fundamental) I. Título. II. Série.

04-2414   CDD-372.652

Índices para catálogo sistemático:
1. Inglês : Ensino fundamental 372.652

ISBN 85-16-04154-9

Reprodução proibida. Art. 184 do Código Penal e Lei 9.610 de 19 de fevereiro de 1998.

Todos os direitos reservados

RICHMOND
EDITORA MODERNA LTDA.
Rua Padre Adelino, 758 — Belenzinho
São Paulo — SP — Brasil — CEP 03303-904
Central de atendimento ao usuário: 0800 771 8181
www.richmond.com.br
2018

Impresso no Brasil

When: Sometime in the distant past...
Where: The fountain-head of a river

There is a fountain-head of clear water in the middle of a forest.

The trees in the forest are tall and beautiful and there are flowers everywhere.

3

The forest is full of different smells and colors. There are yellow bananas and papayas, red mangoes, brown coconuts and yellow pineapples.

There are also many animals and birds. They are free and happy in the trees, on the ground, or near the fountain-head.
The water is clean and fresh.
Everything is in perfect harmony.

Many, many years later...

Look at the water now! It is not a fountain-head. It is a river, big and strong, with many species of fish. And there are small Indian villages along it.

The Indians can swim and fish in the clear water.
They can drink the water too because it is very clean and fresh.
The tribes and the river live in harmony.
The Big River is their friend.

Life is very simple along the Big River.

Sometimes, the river is calm.

Sometimes, there is a flood and the river is violent.

When the river is violent, the Indians go away.

But they are not afraid. They love and respect the river.

When the river is calm, the Indians come back.

The people are explorers. Some of them are friendly, but some are not. Some Indians are slaves now. They are very sad. And they are worried and afraid.

Why are the explorers in the forest?

There is gold in the river.
And there are precious stones — emeralds, rubies and diamonds — in the forest.
The intruders want the gold and the precious stones.

But over the years, more and more strangers come. They come from different countries. They come with their families and friends. Some Indians are worried. They go away. They go into the middle of the forest.

"Good bye, Big River. Good bye, old friend."

Now, there are small towns along the river. But, there are not many trees.

The river is still beautiful, but the water is not very clear.

When: Nowadays...
Where: The Big River

Things are very different now. The Big River is polluted and silent and the water is dirty. There are no trees, no flowers, no animals and no small Indian villages along it.

All we can see are farms, factories and big cities now.

There are many people in the cities and they are not worried about the river.

The Big River is sad now because it is polluted and ugly.

It is dark and smelly. The water is full of garbage.

It is a hot and sunny day. Look at the river! It is almost dry. And it is very dirty.

Look at the people in the city!

"Hey, you guys, water is precious!"

There is no sign of rain.

At this school, the students are tired and thirsty. The teachers are talking to the students. They are worried.

"There is a great waste of water in our homes and in our city, kids."

The students are worried, too.
"Teacher, the river is almost dry and very dirty."
"How can we help?"
"How can we save the river?"

The situation is very serious now. The river is almost dead.

Can the students help?
Can they save the Big River?
What can they do?

All the students can help. Let's see the things they can do.

They can make banners.

They can make pamphlets.

They can talk to their friends.

They can talk to their neighbors.

They can talk to their parents and...

... to their brothers and sisters.

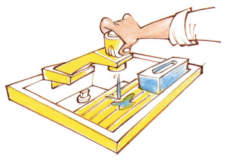

They can do their part.

They can start a campaign.

YEAR: 2050
PLACE: The Big River

Use your imagination. Draw the Big River in 2050.

KEY WORDS

The meaning of each word corresponds to its use in the context of the story (see page number, 00)

afraid (11) com medo
almost (20) quase
along (8) ao longo; acompanhando
because (18) porque
but (8) mas
campaign (27) campanha
city, cities (17) cidade(s)
clean (5) limpa
clear (3) clara
country, countries (14) país(es)
dark (19) escuro
dead (24) morto
dirty (16) suja
do (27) fazer
draw (28) desenhar
dry (20) seco
enemy, enemies (10) inimigo(s)
everything (5) tudo
everywhere (3) em todo lugar
factory, factories (7) fábrica(s)
fish (7) pesca, **(6)** peixe
flood (8) cheia, enchente
fountain-head (3) nascente
free (5) livre
full (4) cheio
garbage (19) lixo
go away (8) ir embora
gold (13) ouro
ground (5) chão
how (23) como
intruder (13) intruso
make (26) fazer
middle (3) meio
near (5) perto
neighbor (27) vizinho

parrot (30) papagaio
parents (26) pais
people (10) pessoas
precious stones (13) pedras preciosas
rattlesnake (30) cascavel
save (23) salvar
sign (20) sinal
slave (11) escravo
smell (4) cheiro
smelly (19) malcheiroso
some (11) alguns
sometimes (8) algumas vezes
still (15) ainda
strong (6) forte
sunny (20) ensolarado
suspicious (10) desconfiados
swim (26) nadar
thirsty (22) com sede
tired (22) cansados
too (23) também
town (15) cidade
ugly (18) feio
want (13) querer
waste (22) desperdício
when (8) quando
who (10) quem
wild cat (30) onça
worried (11) preocupados

Expressions

come back (9) voltar
Hey, you guys! (20) E aí, pessoal!
Let's... (26) Vamos
Nowadays (16) Atualmente

ACTIVITIES

Before Reading

1. Read the front cover of the book. The title is:

   The _____ River

   | Small | | Big |

2. Look at the pictures on pages 4 and 5. Find and circle:

Animal	Fruit
a macaw	a pineapple
a river dolphin	a mango
a wild cat	a coconut

While Reading

3. Read pages 7 to 9 and complete the sentences.
   a) The Indians can _____ and fish in the clear water.
   b) The tribes and the _____ live in harmony.
   c) Sometimes there is a _____ and the river is violent.
   d) They love and _____ the river.

4. Read pages 10 and 11 and match.

   | The Indians are... |

   | The explorers are... |

   suspicious
   slaves
   enemies
   worried
   strange people

30

5. Look at pages 12 and 13. Unscramble the words and complete the sentences.

   a) In the forest there are _____ (birues), _____ (ralemeds) and _____ (dsmondia).

   b) The explorers want the _____ (ldgo) and the _____ (ciouspre snesto).

6. Look at pages 16 and 17. Before you read, compare them with pages 3, 4 and 5. What is different?
   _____

7. Read pages 16 to 19. Tick the correct answers.

   a) Nowadays, the Big River is:
      ( ) big and strong   ( ) polluted and silent
   b) The water is:
      ( ) full of garbage   ( ) clean and fresh

8. Read page 22. Complete the sentences and fill in the crossword.

   a) Kids, in our (1) _____ there is a great (2) _____ of (3) _____.

   b) There is no water. The students are (4) _____ and tired.

Crossword clues filled in:
- 1. _ O _ _
- 2. (down) ends in E
- 3. _ A _ R (across)
- 4. T I R (down, with Y at bottom)

31

9. Look at pages 26 and 27 and complete the table.

HOW CAN THE STUDENTS HELP?

1. They can _____ to their friends.

2. They can _____ their part.

1. They can _____ a campaign.

1. They can _____ pamphlets.

After Reading (Optional Activities)

10. Is there a river in your town/city? Find out about it.

    Name: _____

    Big or Small: _____

    Polluted or Clean: _____

11. Are there campaigns in your town/city for saving water?